THE VAN GOGH COLORING BOOK

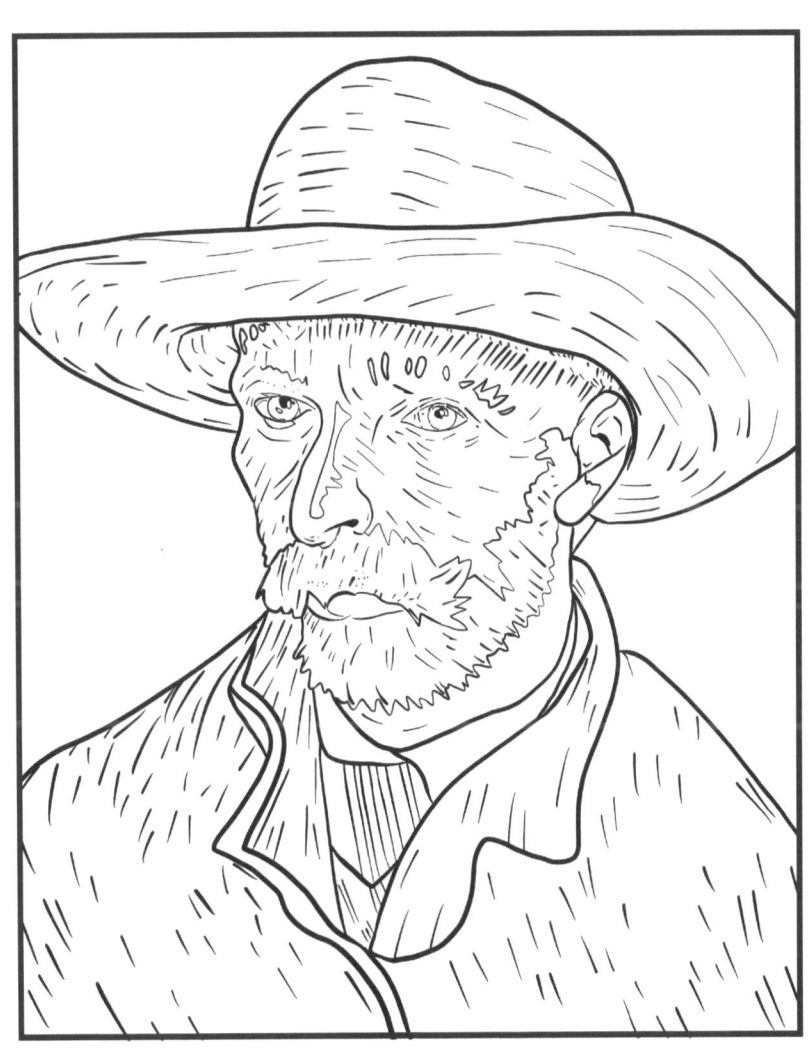

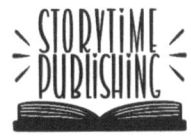

Copyright © 2022 Storytime Publishing

All rights reserved. No part of this book may be reproduced, scanned, or transmitted in any forms, digital, audio, or printed without prior written permission from the author.

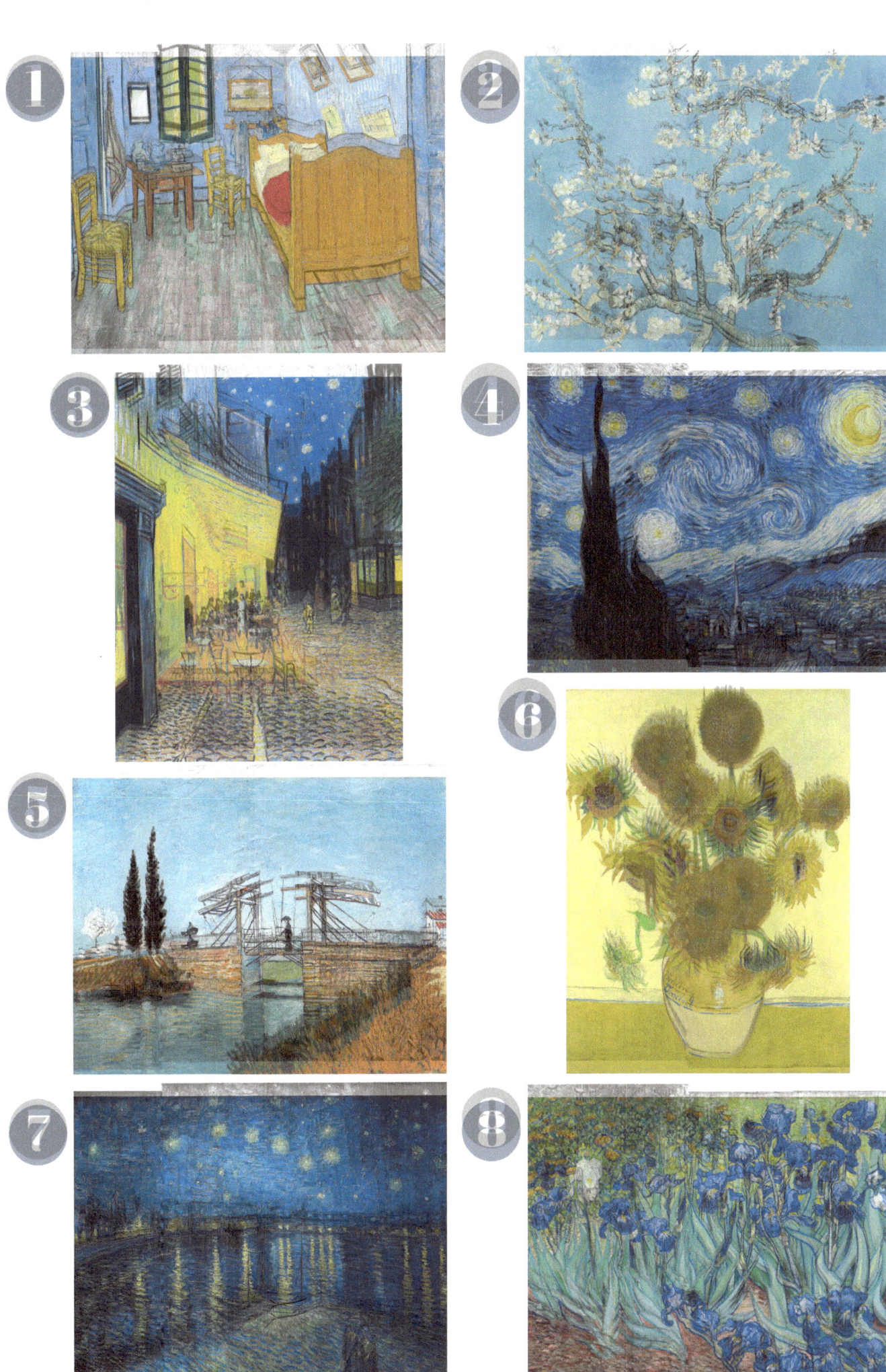

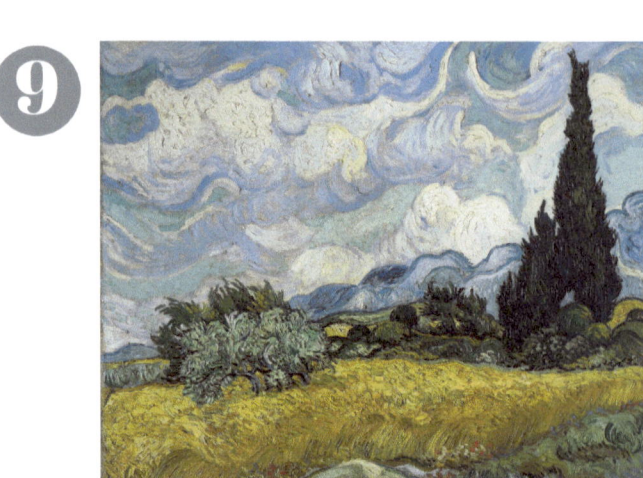

9

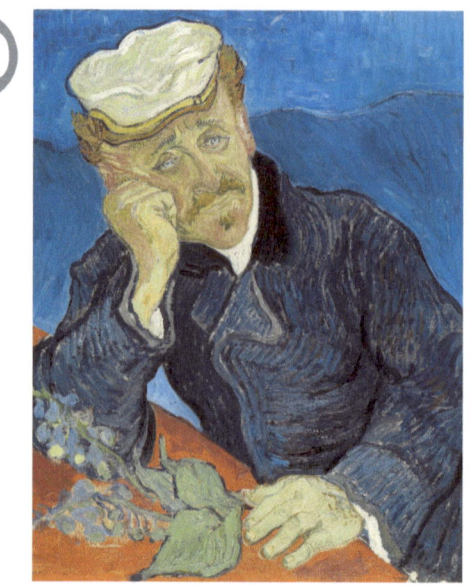

10

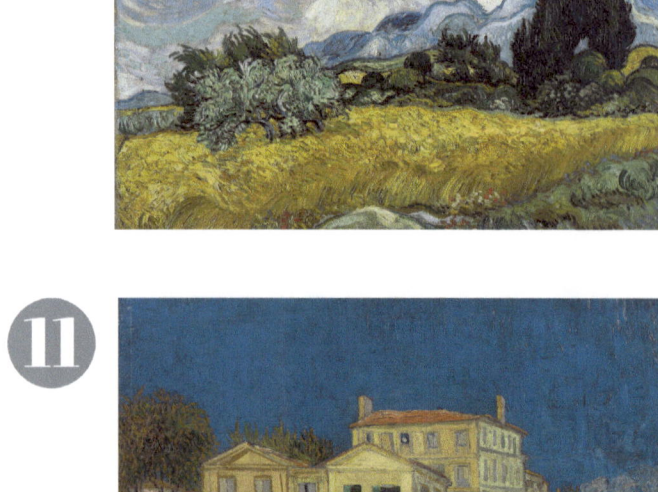

11

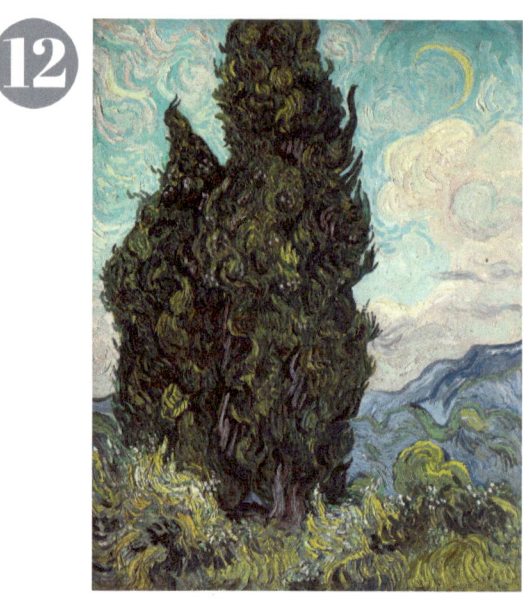

12

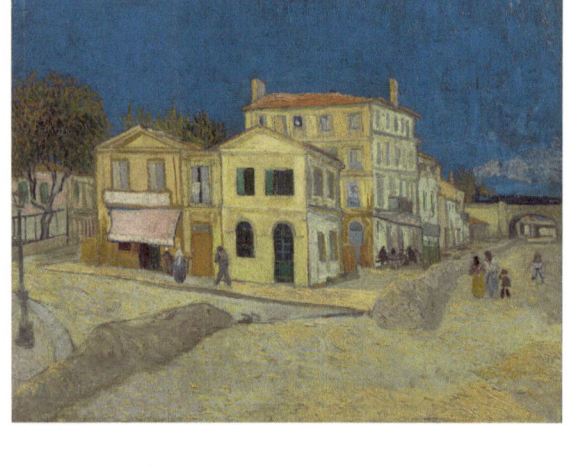

13

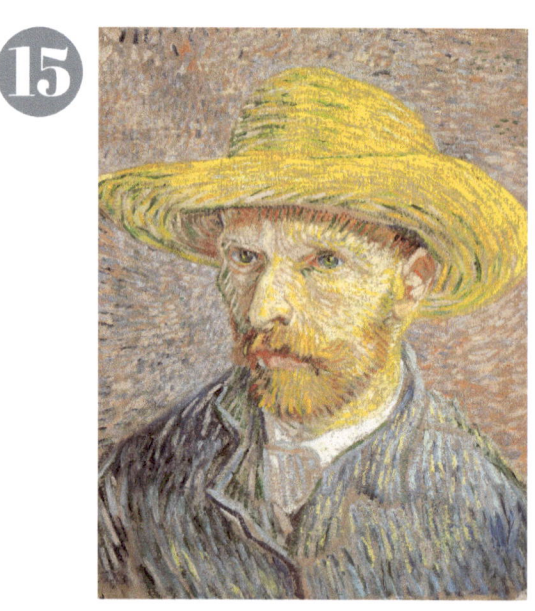

15

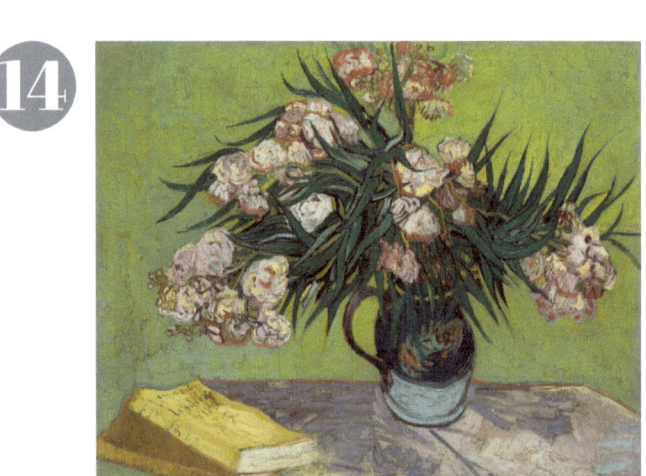

14

"I dream of painting and then I paint my dream."

-Vincent van Gogh

The Bedroom, 1888

Almond Blossoms, 1890

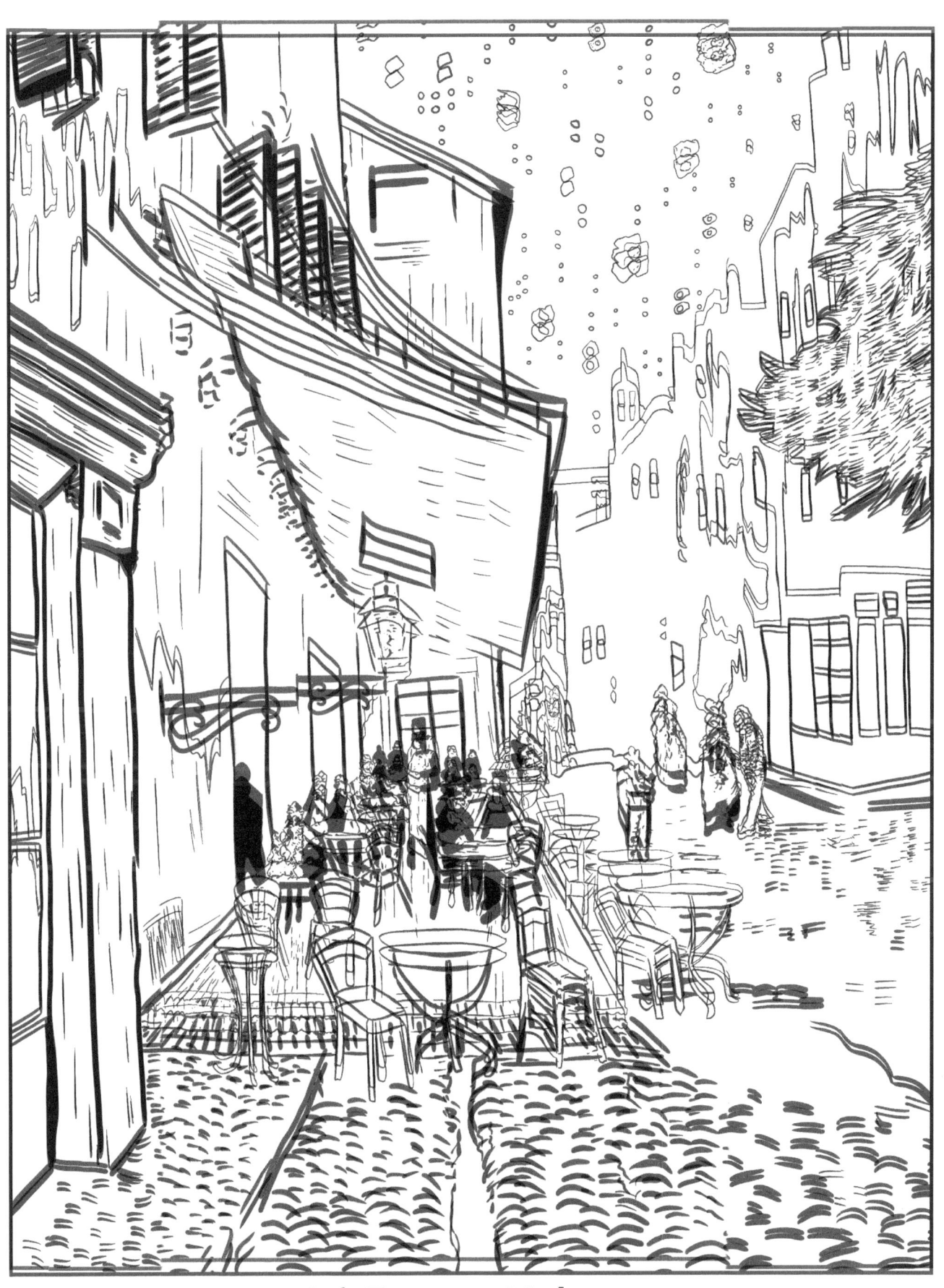

Café Terrace at Night, 1888

The Starry Night, 1889

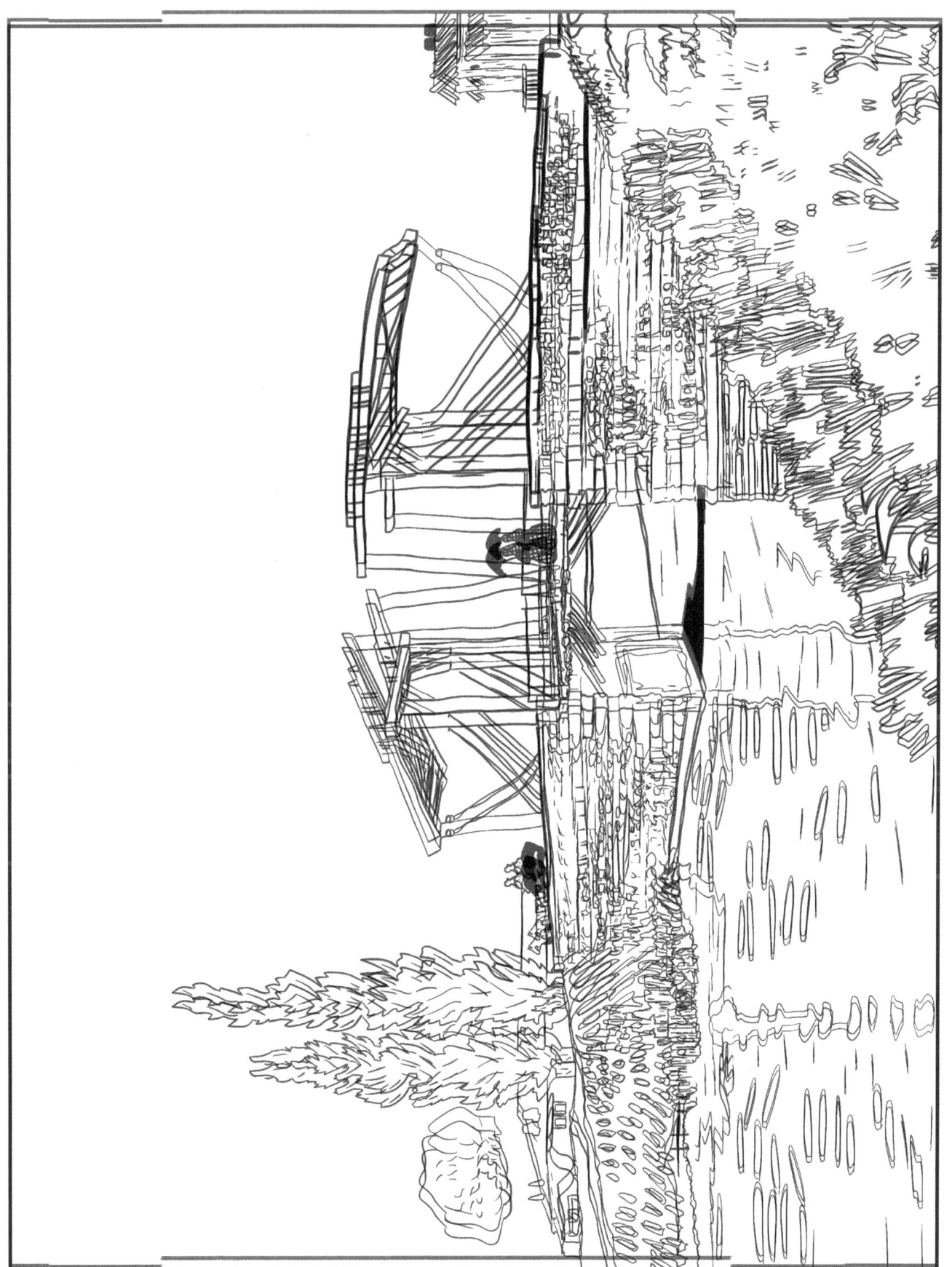

The Langlois Bridge at Arles, 1888

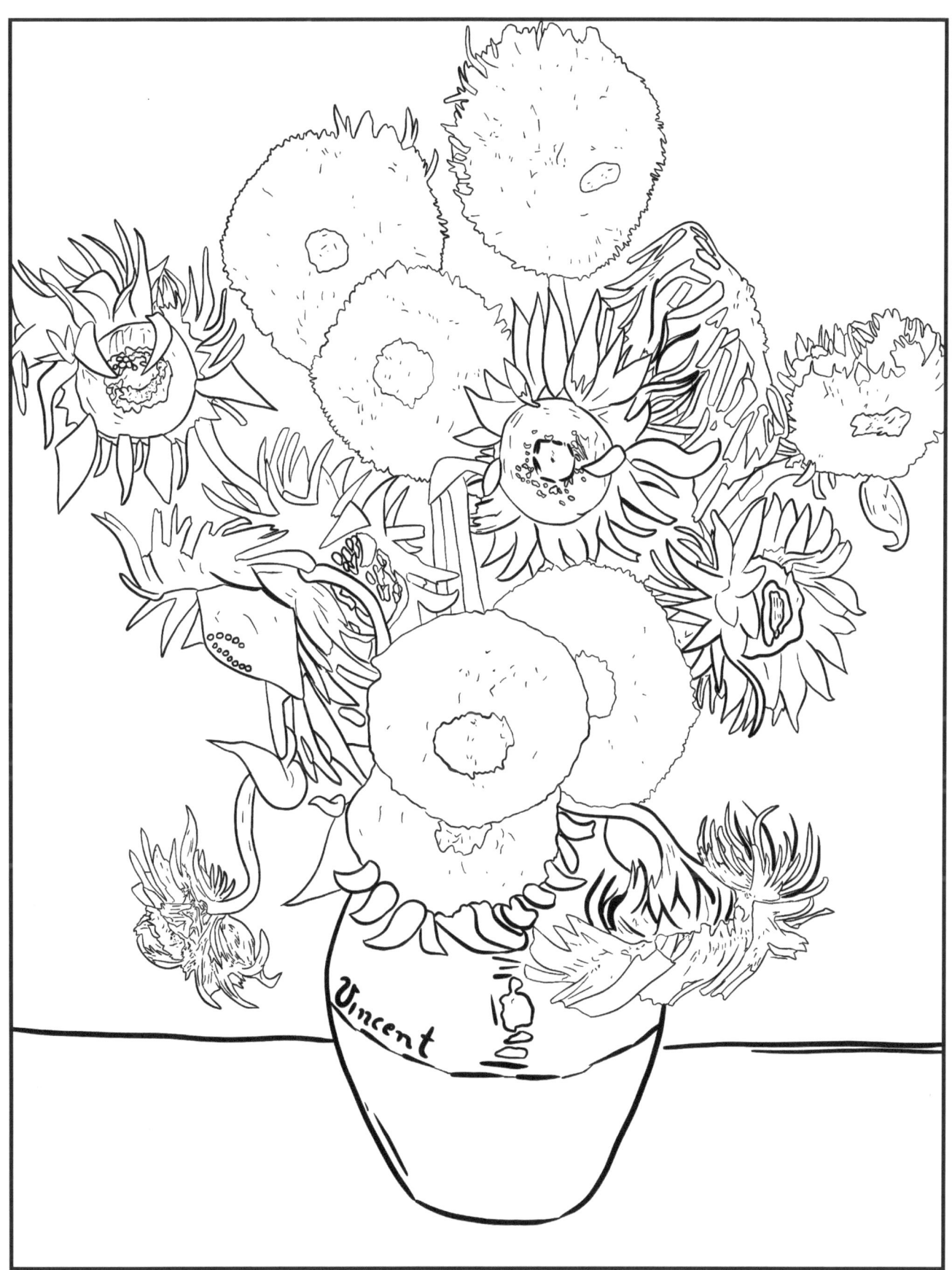

Sunflowers, 1888

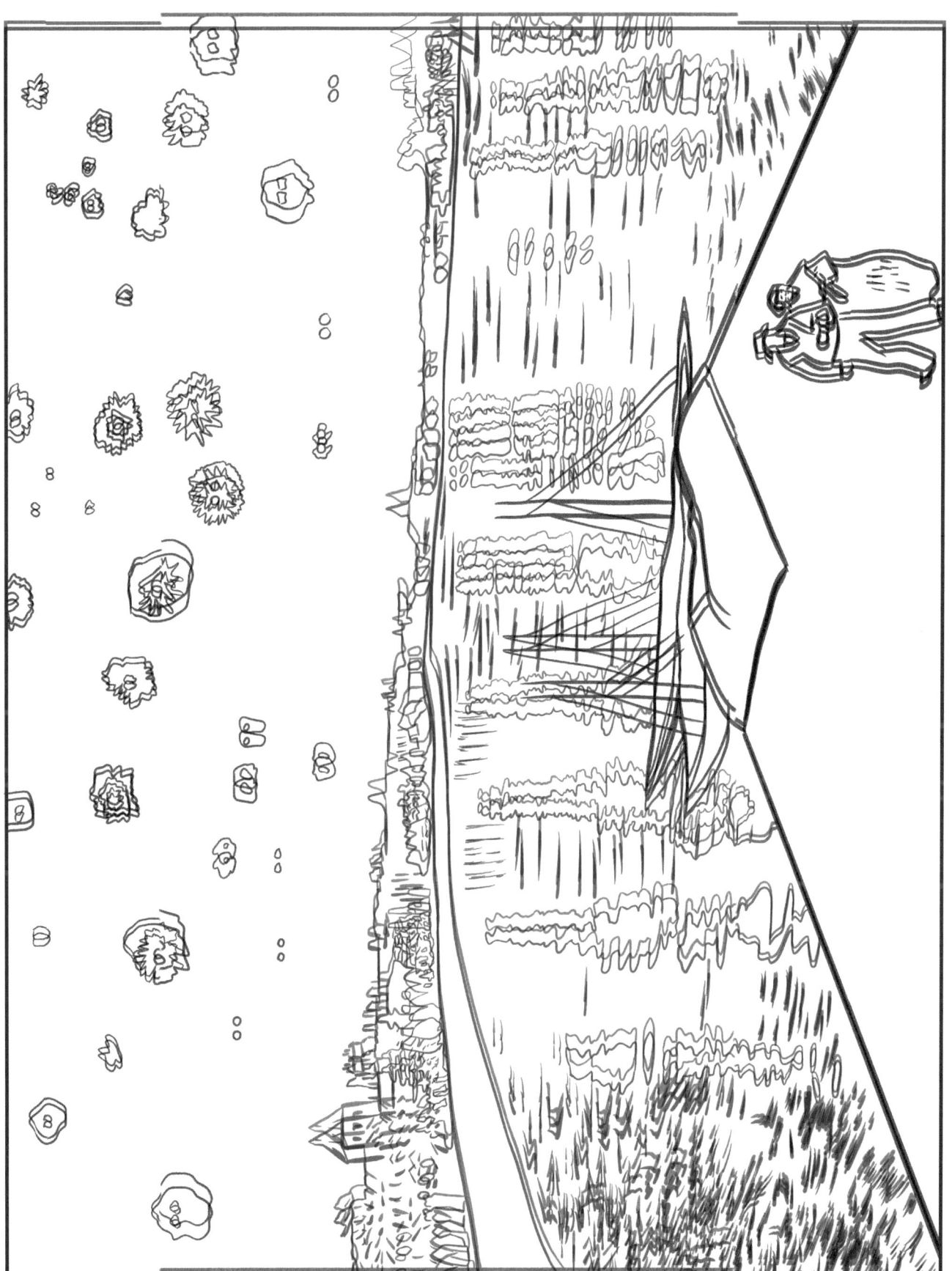

Starry Night Over the Rhône, 1888

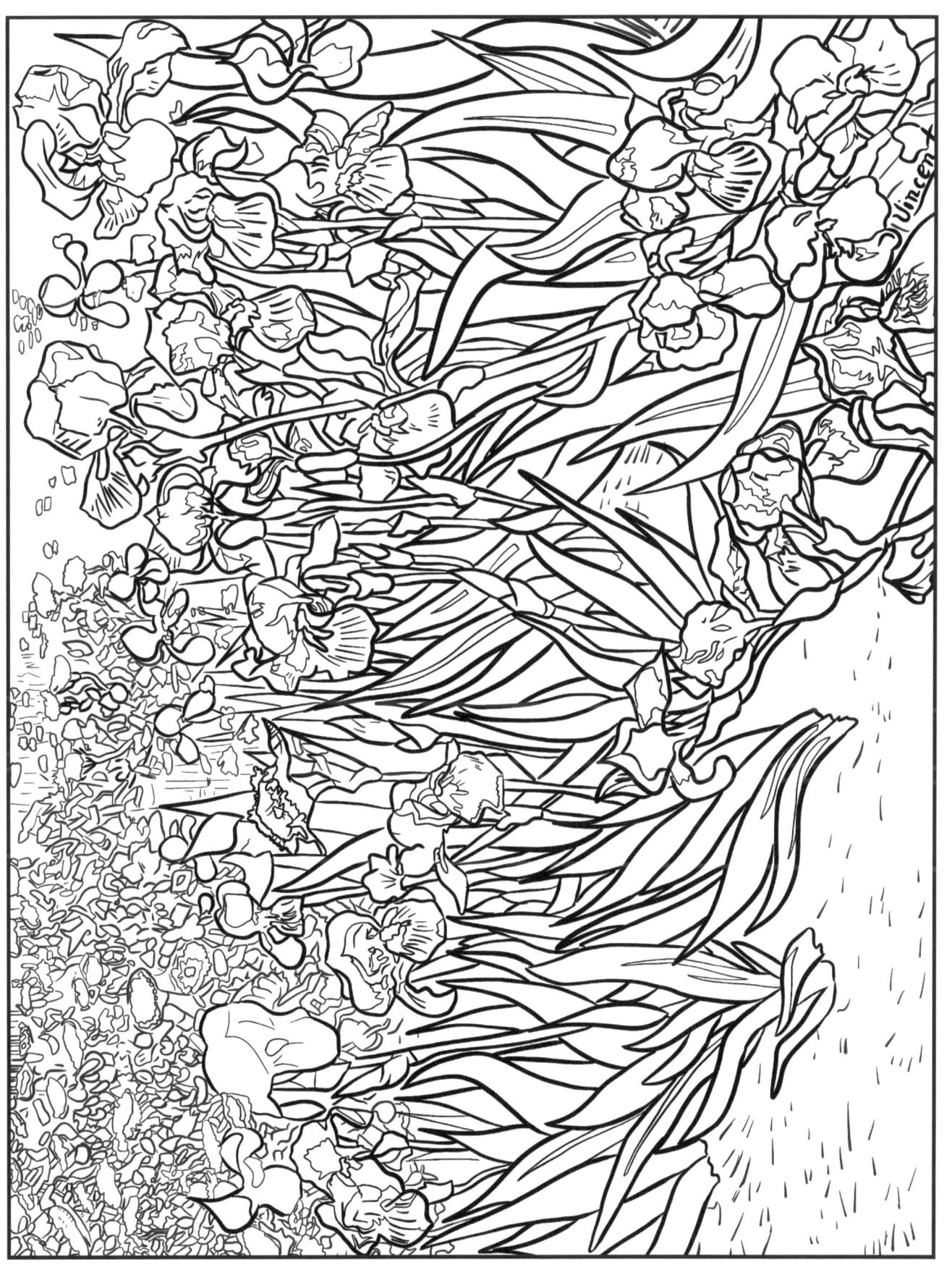

Irises, 1889

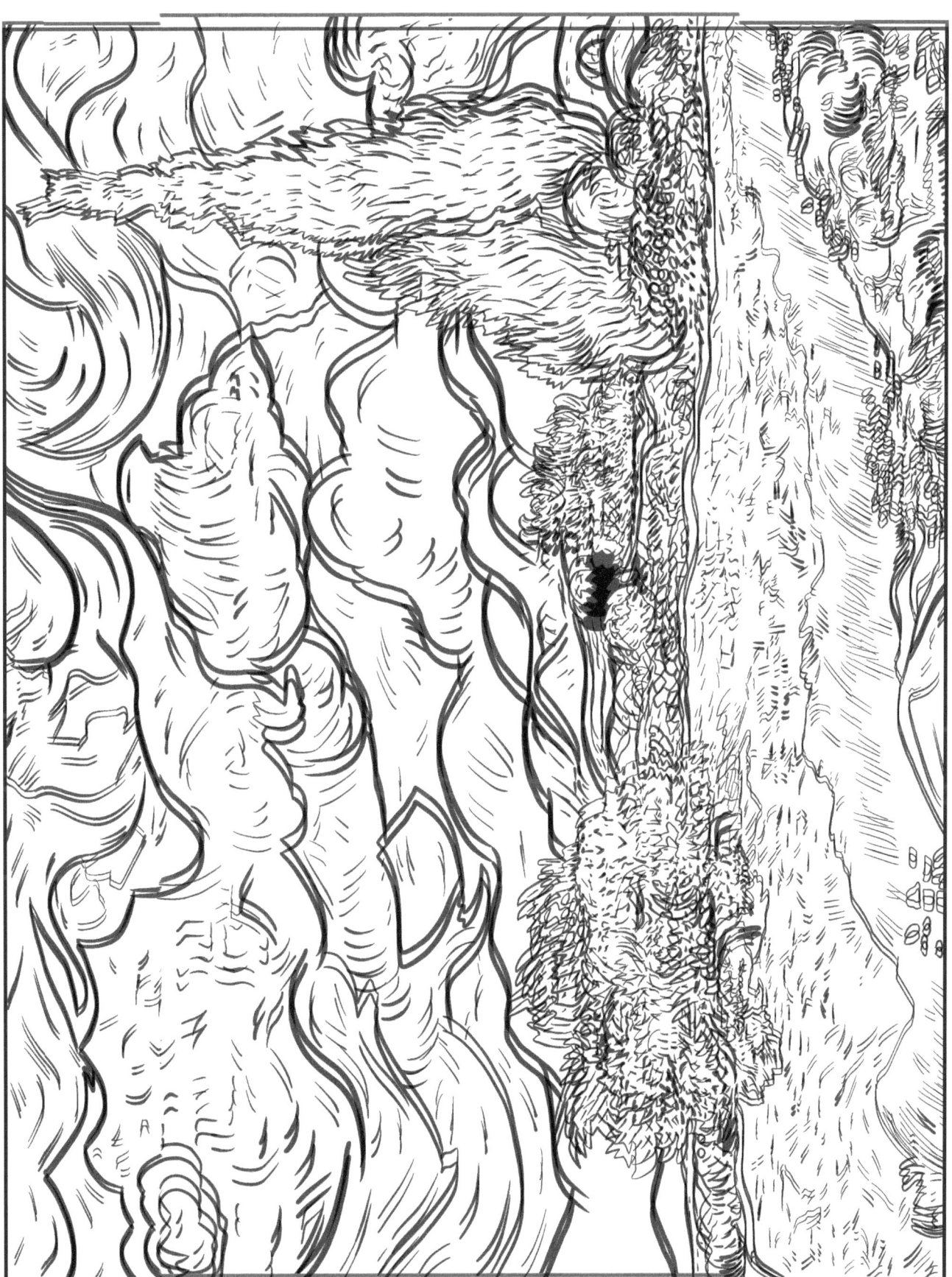

Wheat Field with Cypresses, 1889

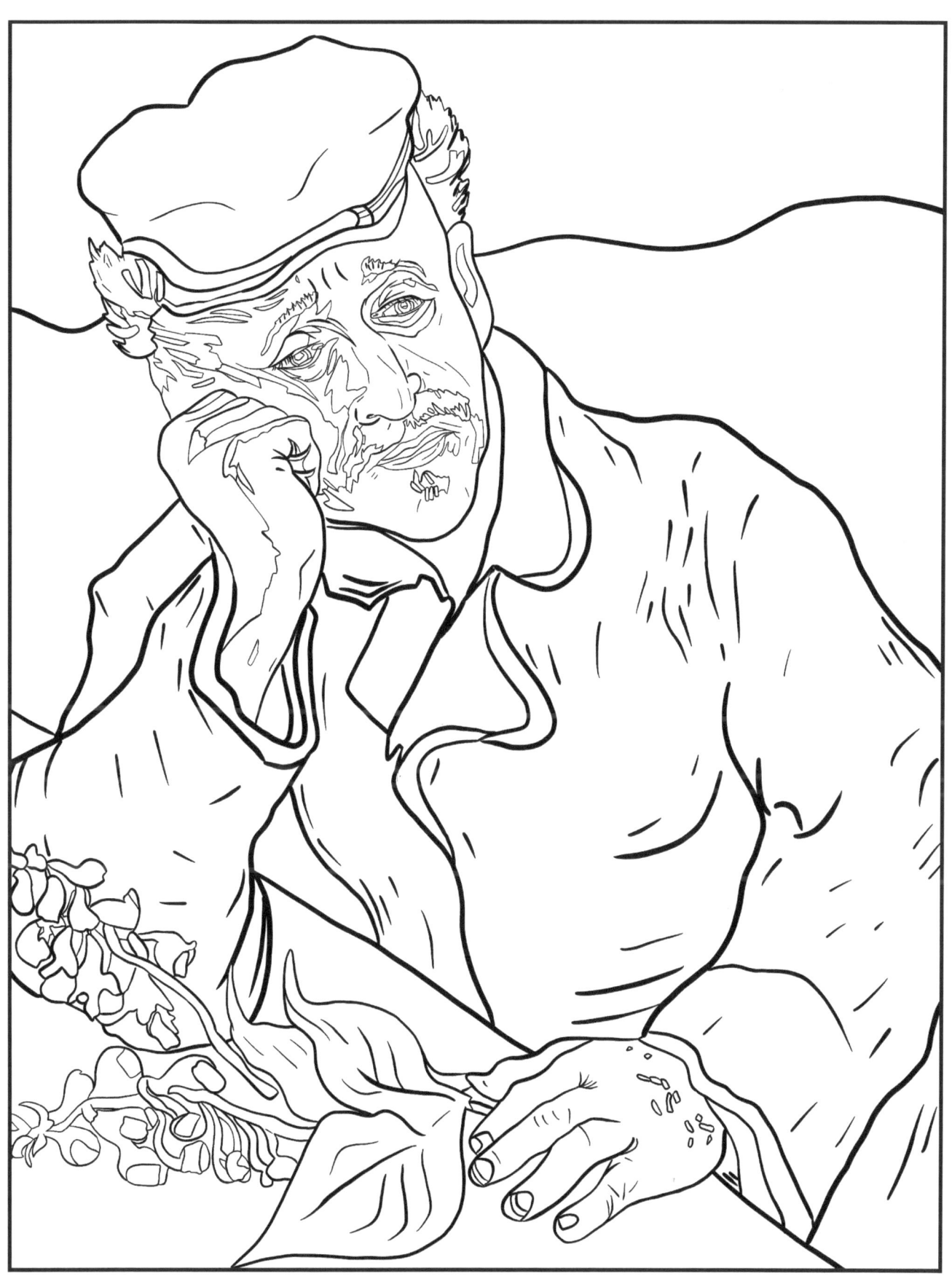

Portrait of Dr. Gachet, 1890

The Yellow House, 1888

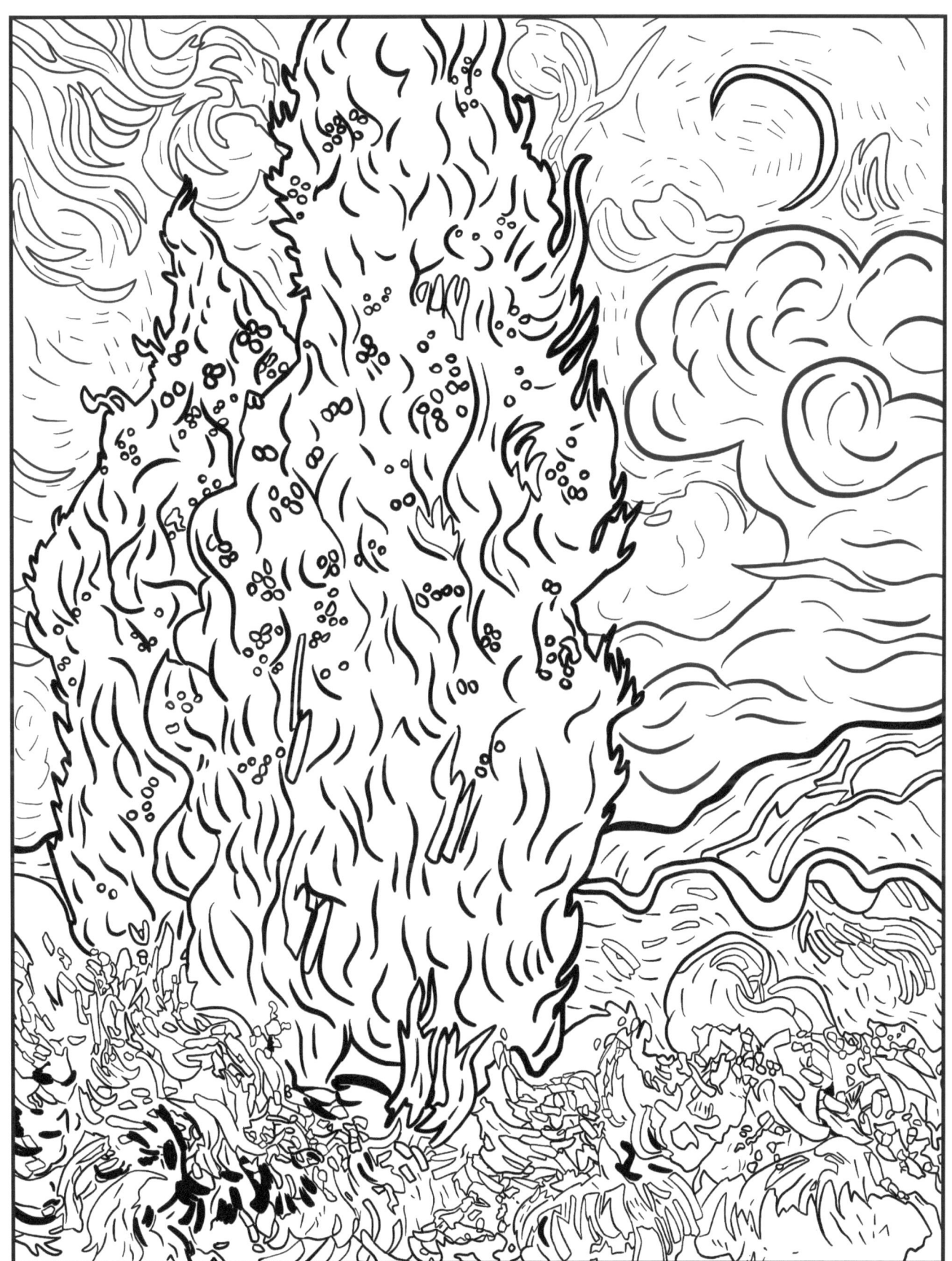

Cypresses, 1889

The Night Café, 1888

Oleanders, 1888

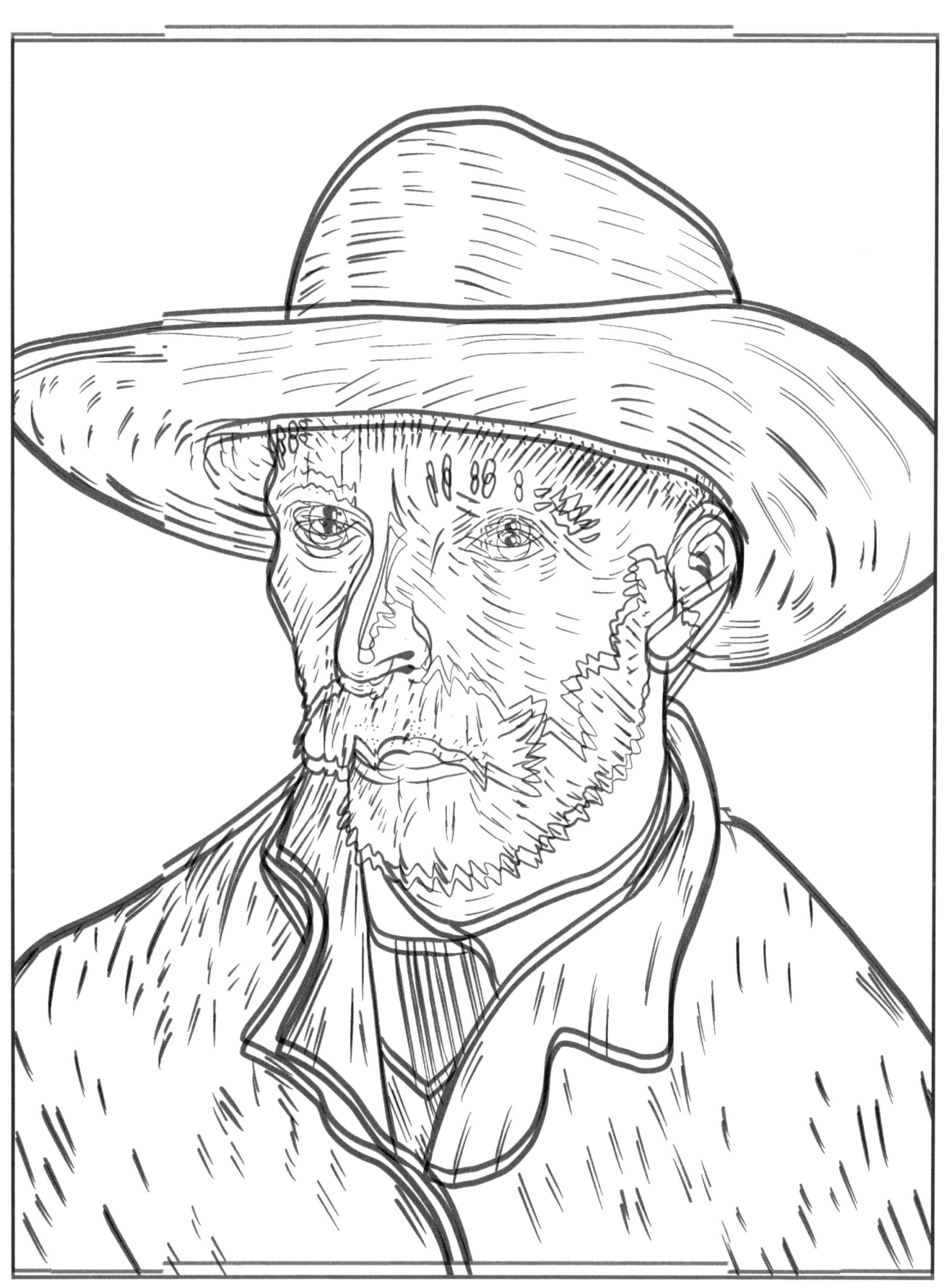

Self-Portrait with a Straw Hat, 1887

www.ingramcontent.com/pod-product-compliance
Lightning Source LLC
Chambersburg PA
CBHW051938210526
45473CB00006B/2294